Animal-watching ⟨...⟩ know what to look for, and how best to observe it. And who better to tell you than author, broadcaster, animal expert and ex-farmer, Dick King-Smith?

There are so many different kinds of animals to see in the British countryside; in wood, field and hedgerow, on moor and mountain. And it's not only the unusual ones that are interesting. Even those animals that are quite commonplace can be exciting to observe – if you know what to look out for.

Country Watch not only tells you what you ought to be looking out for, but it is also crammed with surprising facts about animals. Did you know that the tiny mole can burrow its way through thirty pounds of earth in an hour? Or that a red deer stag sheds its antlers every year in the spring? Or that there are forty-eight different breeds of sheep in the British Isles?

As well as a wealth of fascinating and useful information for animal-watchers, Dick King-Smith provides some wonderful stories about some of the funny, sad and surprising encounters he has had with animals over the years.

Dick King-Smith was a farmer in Gloucestershire for many years and this background has proved invaluable for his amusing animal stories. He also taught in a village primary school but he now writes full time. He has more recently become well-known for his television appearances with his miniature wire-haired dachshund, Dodo, on TV-am's *Rub-a-Dub-Tub* programme.

Dick King-Smith

COUNTRY WATCH

Animals to look out for in the countryside

Illustrated by Catherine Bradbury

PUFFIN BOOKS

Puffin Books, Penguin Books Ltd, Harmondsworth, Middlesex, England
Viking Penguin Inc., 40 West 23rd Street, New York, New York 10010, U.S.A.
Penguin Books Australia Ltd, Ringwood, Victoria, Australia
Penguin Books Canada Ltd, 2801 John Street, Markham, Ontario, Canada L3R 1B4
Penguin Books (N.Z.) Ltd, 182–190 Wairau Road, Auckland 10, New Zealand

First published 1987

Made and printed in Great Britain by
Cox and Wyman Ltd, Reading, Berks

Typeset in 12 on 15 Baskerville by
Rowland Phototypesetting Ltd,
Bury St Edmunds, Suffolk

CONTENTS

Chapter 1

VIEW FROM A HIDE

Just at the moment I have fourteen animals. Three hens, three rabbits, three guinea-pigs and five dogs. One of those dogs, the eldest, is a terrier called Maggie.

Maggie is eleven which means that, since I've had her from a tiny puppy, I've known her for about 4,000 days. But supposing she was lost. Supposing I rang the police station and said, 'I've lost a small terrier,' and they said, 'Could you give us an accurate description of the dog?' Could I?

I could say she was a Jack Russell terrier (the police would recognize that, though actually the great West Country huntsman, Parson Jack Russell, kept terriers of all shapes and sizes). I could say she was black and white with little bits of tan here and there.

'Her head's mostly black,' I'd say, 'and her body white, except for her tail which is half and half. But she does have a distinctive black patch, about the size of a saucer, on one side of her bottom.'

'Which side?' the police might say. And that I couldn't answer.

I'm telling you all this for two reasons. One, to show you I'm someone who's keen on animals. I've always had pets, I used to be a farmer, and I'm very interested in wildlife. The other reason is to try to point out how often we *look* at things – animals, for example, like my Maggie – but don't *see* them.

Seeing animals is what this book's about. There's so much to watch in the countryside, but an awful lot of it you won't notice unless you put your mind (and your eyes) to it.

There are so many different animals to see. All of them are interesting, no matter how ordinary or commonplace.

Some sights and scenes are pleasant – beautiful, exciting, amusing. Some are sad, for death comes daily, and nightly, to a host of creatures in field and wood, on moor and mountain. Some die in the teeth or talons of the hunters. Some are killed – for bad reasons as well as good – by man. Few animals are lucky enough to die peacefully of old age.

Maggie will, I trust, but hopefully not for a long time yet. She doesn't act her age. I've just called her and she's come tearing along like a two year old.

By the way, the black patch is on the right side. I've just looked.

And seen.

One way of seeing without being seen is to build a hide. The dictionary says that a hide is 'a concealed place for observing wild animals'. What it doesn't tell you is that the average hide is cold and damp and pretty uncomfortable.

I'm lucky. My hide is dry and warm and rainproof and draughtproof. That's because my hide is my study, a very small upstairs-room in my old cottage, and I can sit at my desk and look out of the window and observe animals – wild and tame – all day long.

Well, not all day long, or I'd never get any writing done, but I do seem to spend a lot of time staring out, at the little paddock below me that runs down to the stream, at the field that rises beyond it, a steepish field called Burr Acre, and, beyond that, at the distant hills that are the very southernmost end of Cotswold.

I don't expect to see any very rare or extraordinary animals. I simply find that watching living creatures is interesting, however common they may be. Just now, for example, there's a big gang of starlings strutting about in their busybody way, working over the bitten grass of the paddock.

The Friesian herd from Church Farm is grazing its way out after morning milking, and the starlings snap up the insects that the beasts disturb and also find interesting bits of grub in the cowpats.

starling

Starlings are flock birds (there's safety in numbers), and they eat absolutely anything and never stop working, which is why they are such successful animals. Some people think of them as just dull blackish birds, but, looked at carefully, their glossy feathering has beautiful sheens of purple and green, speckled with white and buff tips in winter.

That's really what this book is about – looking carefully at animals and their actions. There's so much animal behaviour going on around us every day that we never notice. Sometimes there are scenes of comedy, sometimes of high drama, sometimes of tragedy. But there's almost always something of interest to see.

At this moment I can see something from my hide that's interesting, because there is a strange coincidence about it.

One of the cows in the dairy herd has lost the lower half of her tail, in an accident perhaps. Maybe she got it caught somewhere, and it became infected and dropped off, leaving her without a hairy switch to lash at the flies. What's left of the tail looks comical as she flips it about ineffectually.

But here's the coincidence. Hopping along behind the cow is another black and white animal, a magpie. And it too has lost its tail – how I don't know, though perhaps my neighbour's cat does. Magpies have very long tails, as long as the rest of their bodies, and the loss has quite upset this bird's balance. Even its hops are clumsy, and now, as something disturbs it, it has to work terribly hard to keep its tailless body airborne. It too looks comical, like a fluttery old black and white hen, but unlike the cow, whose loss hardly affects her, this magpie may well not make old bones. A tragic end is never far away for a handicapped creature.

I can still see the tailless cow as she munches her way up Burr Acre, but I wonder if I shall see the magpie again.

I'll have to keep my eyes peeled.

'Hopping along behind the cow is another black and white animal, a magpie.'

Chapter 2

IN THE FIELDS

It's very difficult to stand in a field and *not* see any animals, because even if there appears to be nothing on the ground, a look at the sky will almost always show you some birds on the wing.

For example, in summer there are sure to be swallows hawking for insects, flying high on fine days and skimming low over the grass if the weather has changed for the worse. You won't see them in winter of course. They leave for South Africa at the end of September and don't return till the end of April. Many other birds migrate. Some, like the cuckoo, and the swallows' cousins, the swifts and the martins, leave us for the winter, going south to find warmer weather. Others come down from the north to spend the winter with us: like the redwings and fieldfares from Scandinavia, and many swans and geese from Arctic Russia and Greenland.

The amazing thing about long-distance migration is not only the fact that birds travel thousands of miles from one part of the world to another. How do they do it? How do they navigate? How will the swallow that builds a nest in the garage roof and whose family's droppings splatter the top of my car find its way back, to that exact spot, next year?

There is a record of a bird called a Manx Shearwater that was taken from its burrow (shearwaters nest in burrows) on the island of Skokholm, off the west coast of Wales. It was ringed, and flew (in an aeroplane) across the Atlantic to America. Then it was released at Boston Airport. Twelve and a half days later that shearwater was back at Skokholm, having flown 5000 kilometres!

There doesn't seem to be a simple answer to the question of how migrant birds solve these very difficult navigational problems. Adults, who have done the trip before, may recognize landmarks, but how do juveniles manage? How does a migrating youngster a few months old, with a brain the size of your thumbnail, find its way to, let's say, South Africa?

There's evidence that birds use the sun and the stars as navigation beacons, but then suppose they're flying in thick fog? They must somehow be aware of the earth's magnetic field. But then again, how do they compensate for drift in strong winds, and for time-changes?

There don't seem to be any easy answers.

However in winter, when the swallows are sunning themselves thousands of miles away, there are plenty of native birds to catch your eye – those old starlings of course, and many small birds as well as bigger ones such as woodpigeons and magpies, or rooks and carrion crows.

But just supposing that for a moment you couldn't see a single living creature in the air or on the ground, never forget that under your feet, under the grass of that field, there are hundreds of thousands of a very important kind of animal that plays a vital part in the growth of that good green grass you're standing on. And the name of that animal? The earthworm.

Next time you see a worm, spare a moment to think what a marvellous beast it is. As it bores and burrows its way through the soil, it loosens and perforates it, letting in air, letting in the rain that nourishes the roots of plants, and makes it easier for those roots to grow down and feed. It even provides a lot of the food that a plant needs, by pulling leaves and straws and stalks down into the earth. And, to cap it all, the worm is a kind of miniature dung-spreader because the way it 'eats' is to pass soil through the length of its body. It removes what it needs as food and discharges the rest in the shape of wormcasts, which make fine manure for grass and grain.

It's been estimated that every year, on every acre of land, worms recycle ten tons of new soil, so you can see that there must be quite a few of them about, something for which about half the birds in this country are very grateful, not to mention a lot of mammals. Hedgehogs, for example, foxes, and above all badgers eat masses and masses of earthworms. It must be like stuffing yourself with long, thin, pink chipolata sausages.

A long, long time ago, I had a friend called Tom, who ate a worm for a dare. Then – luckily – for another dare he ate a potful of mustard, which made him very sick. It served Tom right, but it can't have been much fun for the poor old worm.

In every field in the country two things have changed dramatically since those distant days when Tom and I were boys.

First, there are no elm trees. Once every hedgerow had its rank of tall shady elms but Dutch elm
disease has killed them all. Dutch elm disease is so
called because it once almost wiped out the elms of
Holland. The cause of it is the Elm Bark Beetle,
who lives on the starches and sugars under the
bark of this tree. If you pull off a flap of diseased
bark, you'll see the creature's parallel galleries
underneath. The beetle carries a fungus which is
the cause of the disease. There was an outbreak in
this country in the 1920s, from which the elm
population partially recovered, but a far worse
outbreak in the 1970s did for them all.

The second change is this. The commonest wild
animal of our boyhood, the one creature we'd have
been certain to see in any and every field, has now
become much rarer. That animal is the rabbit,
once almost wiped out by the plague called
myxomatosis.

There are still quite a lot of rabbits about of
course, colonies grown resistant to the disease, but
only yesterday I took the train to London and
back, perhaps two hundred miles in all. Years ago
I would have seen thousands of rabbits in the
course of the journey. Yesterday, I saw one.

The rabbit was introduced by the Normans in
the late 1300s. At that time, and for some hundreds
of years after, the animal was called a 'coney' (only

'Once every hedgerow had its rank of tall shady elms . . .'

'. . . but Dutch elm disease has killed them all.'

the young were known as rabbits) and kept in a 'coneygarth' – a word coming from 'coney' and 'earth'.

Later, a coneygarth became known as a warren.

A warren was a specially chosen area, fenced off or sometimes walled in to keep rabbits in and predators out, often with artificial burrows constructed by the warrener. It was his job to breed as many as possible for food. Of course lots escaped, and before long there was a huge and ever-growing wild population. Rabbits became a pest. To the farmer especially the rabbit was a menace. It dug its holes everywhere, it stripped the bark from young trees, and it helped itself to his crops. On the headlands of every field the grass or young corn would be nibbled away for yards from each hedge inward, and rabbits died in hordes before gun and dog and ferret, in gin-traps and in snares. Before 1953, a hundred million rabbits were killed in Britain every year!

Then came myxomatosis, and the animal that had provided a good meal for scores of generations of countrymen practically disappeared.

'Good riddance!' said the farmers, and it's hard to blame them when you think of the millions of pounds worth of damage that the pretty, cuddly, little bunny-rabbit did to their crops every year. But the disease that came was a horrible one, bringing a slow and lingering death.

Let's just hope that now a balance has been struck, so that we may continue to see a good few rabbits hopping about our countryside. But not too many!

An animal of the fields which you may well come upon is the hare.

The hare doesn't live in a burrow like the rabbit. It's a solitary animal that lies above ground, crouching flat on the grass in a slight depression called a 'form'. It sits so still that you may very nearly tread upon it. Only a few days ago I was walking down a slope following my German Shepherd dog, Sam, who has a marvellous 'nose' (a very good sense of smell), and he passed within six feet of a hare that lay so motionless and gave out, it seems, so little scent that he had no idea it was there.

As soon as he had passed, the hare got to its feet, right beside me as I followed, and loped off up the hill, still unseen by the dog.

Sam's eyes, like those of all predators or hunters of prey, face forwards so that he can see what he is chasing. The eyes of a creature that expects to be hunted, like a hare, are set on each side of the head, so that 'puss', as huntsmen call this animal, can look back and see its pursuer. Why 'puss', I don't know. Some say that the Latin word for hare, 'lepus', was Frenchified into 'le pus', but I don't think I want to take their word for that! A number of hares are killed on the roads at night, for instead of dodging into the safety of the hedge, they run straight on, keeping their eyes fixed on the great glaring ones of the car behind.

Unlike the rabbit, the hare is a native British animal. And it is indeed unlike the rabbit in several ways. It is larger, taller, has longer ears that are black-tipped, and longer legs. Its hind-legs in particular are very powerful, and it can run extremely fast, much too fast for a dog like Sam. I never worry when he chases a hare because I know he hasn't a hope of catching it and will come puffing back to me before long.

Some dogs, however, kill hares, and indeed there are two kinds that are bred for just such 'sport'.

One is the beagle, a miniature hound, with a marvellous nose to stick to the line of a hunted hare, and the stamina to keep steadily on until at last the speedy hare is exhausted. For myself, I don't approve of the idea of a pack of thirty or so beagles pitted against so beautiful and harmless a creature as a hare, but I'm even less keen on another blood sport, where another breed of dog, the greyhound, is used for hare-hunting, or coursing.

On the beagling field the hare has at least a fair chance of escape but the sport of coursing is a different matter. It involves a pair of tremendously fast greyhounds chasing a hare, and no matter how it dodges and doubles and jinks, its death is a certainty.

Listen to the cries of a hare being killed and you may, like me, set your face against both these blood sports.

In March you may see hares 'boxing' – standing upright and jumping around on their hind-legs, jabbing at one another with their forefeet. It used to be thought that only the jacks (the males) did this, but now it is known that the slightly larger females, the does, box too, in this mating season.

The babies, called leverets for their first year, are born above ground, and if you should stumble upon one crouching still as a stone, leave it alone. Once we found a leveret, and then, fifty yards away, another. Thinking that they had been deserted by their mother, we picked them up and put them in an empty rabbit-hutch. My wife fed them

warm cows' milk through a fountain-pen-filler every few hours for days on end. But weeks later, both babies suddenly died. In fact, we had killed them, out of misplaced kindness. There had been nothing wrong with them when we'd found them. The doe had placed them well apart, for safety, and would have come back to each in turn to feed it.

Remember this story if you should find a leveret, or indeed any baby animal that seems lost. Don't be tempted to pick up the baby blackbird or the

23

young starling that has tumbled out of its nest. The parents will still look after it, and continue to feed it until it's strong enough to fly. There's a chance that the cat may get it of course, but a much bigger chance that if you adopt it, it will die despite your well-meant help. Leave it alone. Hundreds of years ago, many country people left the hare severely alone. Superstition said that the devil took the shape of a hare, and a pregnant woman especially would very much hope that one didn't cross her path. If it did, she feared her child when born would have a harelip.

Poor old hare – shot by 'sportsmen', hunted, coursed.

Leave it alone, and enjoy the sight of it running free on those long legs.

There are many other four-legged animals that you might see in the fields, but there's one very interesting animal that you almost certainly won't because, like the worms, it lives underground. This is the mole.

You can see where a mole has been, by the casts of earth that it throws up in its ceaseless search for food, principally those same worms. All the year round it hunts them (it's too busy to hibernate), digging its way along with its powerful spade-shaped forefeet, and then turning round and

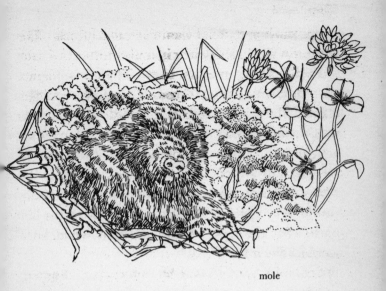

mole

pushing the earth back down the tunnel till it erupts into a molehill. A mole, it has been estimated, can shift thirty pounds of earth in an hour! No wonder there are a lot of people who wish it would do its digging in a wood instead of under their lawns or golf courses or bowling-greens.

If you find a specially large molehill, this is the mole's base, called its 'fortress', and here, at times of good hunting, it stores spare worms, biting them first to cripple them so that they can't escape.

The mole's eyesight is extremely poor, but its sense of smell is acute and it is very sensitive to touch and vibration. The hairs on its velvety coat are all set vertically so that they will lie flat as it works, no matter which way it goes.

Once I had a moleskin waistcoat, beautifully warm and soft. I never troubled to think how many moles had died to provide it.

You might just be lucky and see the earth move as the mole tunnels, even perhaps see a snout poke out. Certainly there are sharper eyes than yours that would notice not just the movement of a mole but the whisk of a fieldmouse and even the trudge of a beetle. Those eyes would belong to the kestrel, hanging above at its 'pitch', motionless save for the quiver of its wing-tips. 'Windhover' is another of its names, as is 'mouse-hawk', though in fact the kestrel belongs not to the hawk family but to the falcons. Falcons are the long-winged types of these birds of prey. Also they do not construct nests, whereas hawks make large, clumsy ones. It's a job to tell by looking upwards, but if you see a kestrel at perch, there's a colour difference between male and female. Both are chestnut-brown, but the cock bird has a grey head and tail. One good place to see the kestrel is by the side of a boring old motorway. There are lots of good things for it to catch and eat on the verges or on the embankments, and it's really quite difficult to make a motorway journey without seeing this bird.

Sometimes, as the kestrel flaps its way from one hunting-ground to another, it has to put up with some unwelcome attention. The carrion crow, a much larger and more powerful bird, thinks kestrel-teasing an amusing game, and often a pair of crows will pester the little falcon unmercifully, diving at it in turn with deep croaks of crow-laughter until it is forced to seek shelter in the depths of a tree. And it isn't only kestrels that crows like to torment. At this very moment I can see from my hide a pair swooping at one of the Church Farm collies as she crosses Burr Acre. She stands on her hind-legs and snaps at them as they shoot over her.

Carrion crows and rooks are two of the three members of the crow family that you're most likely to see about the fields. It's easy to tell them apart.

The carrion crow is a solitary bird, usually seen flying alone or in pairs, while rooks are sociable animals, feeding and flying in large numbers and building their nests all together, in rookeries. Sometimes a whole cluster of rooks will gather in a tree-top, all shouting at the tops of their voices. Perhaps because that's how MPs behave, this is called a rooks' parliament. Actually it's probably caused by one rook trying to steal the sticks from another's nest, while everyone else cheers or

rookery

curses. The other, most obvious difference between rook and crow is that the latter bird is all
black, while the rook has a bare white patch at the
base of its bill.

The third one of the crow tribe which you're
bound to notice, because of its flashy colouring and
its noisy chatter, is the magpie.

You won't see a flock of magpies in large numbers like rooks, but you may see enough to remember the old Scottish rhyme:

> One's sorrow, two's mirth,
> Three's a wedding, four's a birth,
> Five's a christening, six a dearth,
> Seven's heaven, eight is hell,
> And nine's the devil his ane sel'.

As I write, I can see one (oh dear!), but wait, here's
a second (ha, ha!). They're exploring the trough in
the paddock below for any bits of food the cows
might have left. Always, between pecks, they're on
the look-out, long tails flirting, heads turning this
way and that, sharp eyes searching everywhere for
danger.

A very clever bird the magpie is, always on the
go, always watchful, eating everything and anything, ever curious, especially about bright shiny
things which it likes to steal. Though I've never

magpie

met one, I believe that tamed youngsters can be taught to speak.

I wonder how my friend with no tail is getting on?

Magpies are easy to spot from a distance because of their brilliant black and white plumage and their noisiness, though they will only allow you so close and no closer before taking wing. That distance is round about thirty-five yards, the extreme range of a shotgun blast. And the clever crow of course is the same, very careful to keep just far enough away.

I sold my shotguns a long time ago – I don't like shooting things any more. But I can remember the last crow that I did shoot, who wasn't quite careful enough.

I had a lot of guinea-pigs in an open run on my back lawn. They had a house to run into if danger threatened, but every day there seemed to be one less. I kept watch from an upstairs window (another hide) and after a while saw a big carrion crow drop down into the run. Into their house scuttled the guinea-pigs. The crow hopped up and stood beside the door and waited. Before very long a little guinea-pig poked his head out, and you can guess what happened.

Later that afternoon, I hid in a nearby loose-box, gun in hand. The crow came back, and you can guess what happened.

There's another bird of the fields that's much harder to see than the sable crow or the gaudy magpie, because of its protective colouring and its habit of crouching still or running bent low through the grass cover. And that is the partridge, which may well give you a shock by getting up right under your feet, and exploding away in a whirring flight that is a mixture of quick wingbeats and glides. Partridges have their own collective noun (a word used to describe a number of animals of the same sort – a 'herd' of cows, a 'flock' of

partridge

sheep). We speak of a 'covey' of partridges. You may hear them at dusk – 'Keric-eric-eric-eric!' they cry.

It's a loud harsh noise, very different from the clear bubbling song of a much smaller bird of the open lands, the skylark.

The skylark, unlike a lot of birds, sings a long song, perhaps for twenty minutes of an hour; and because there are no perches in the middle of a field, the skylark's perch is the sky. On the ground it does not hop, it walks or runs; but to sing, it climbs high into the blue and hovers, and climbs again, drifts down and then climbs once more, singing away all the time.

Its song is a beautiful, joyful one, and though we

know that the main reason for birdsong is to proclaim a territory, it's nice to think, as the poets always have, that the skylark sings simply because it's happy.

There's another bird that's easy to recognize, because it will introduce itself to you by telling you its name. 'Pee-wit!' it cries.

Actually it has two other names, green plover

peewit

and lapwing (which I imagine was once 'flapwing', because of its very distinctive flight, flapping its heavy rounded wings in a deliberate manner).

It makes no proper nest but lays its eggs in a slight hollow on the ground; if you happen to walk too near, the peewit will swoop and twirl and roll over your head, crying its name wildly as it tries to draw you away. Often in winter you'll see large flocks of lapwings standing around on ploughed ground.

Land under the plough doesn't interest the last common bird of the fields that I'm going to tell you about, the woodpigeon.

The woodpigeon eats a variety of things, but the time it likes best is when those ploughed fields have been sown with corn, and it can feast on the young, sprouting, green grain.

It's a bit like the ordinary town pigeon to look at, but much bigger, with a white mark on its neck and a large white bar on each wing, easy to see as it flies. Often in flight the woodpigeon swoops up to a height, claps its strong-feathered wings together, and then swoops down again. It's a very distinctive motion, as though the bird was breasting a steep invisible wave in the sky and then surfing down the other side of it.

Of course there is a host of other animals – mammals, birds and insects – that you might see during a walk in the fields. I've only mentioned a few, ones that you are likely to see (leaving out the mole and the worm!).

Let's follow the woodpigeon, as it lives up to its name and flies back to its nest – in the wood.

wood pigeon

Chapter 3

IN THE WOODS

You may not be able to see the woodpigeon's nest, a flattish platform of sticks in the depths of a tree or bush, but you can't fail to hear the noise that the bird makes. The song has five notes – 'Co-*coo*-coo, *coo-coo*', and it ends with a sixth, a short 'cuk', as though the pigeon had been suddenly interrupted.

'Co-*coo*-coo, *coo-coo*, cuk' – it's a drowsy noise of hot summer days, and indeed there's seldom silence in a wood, no matter what time of year it is. Somewhere some bird will be saying something.

Spring brings new voices, of the chiffchaff and the willow warbler, and all through the winter the robin sings his clear sad song. In winter too, though the songbirds' season is over, there is always noise in the woods – the harsh croak of the crow, the chatter of the magpie, the screech of the jay and the laughter of the green woodpecker. At dusk you can hear the 'chink-chink-chink!' alarm call of the blackbird, and at night there are the owls.

The jay is a particularly handsome woodland bird, brilliantly coloured, with blue and black bars on each wing, and a pinkish body with white rump and black tail. It has a crest that it can raise, and a piercing scream of a voice. Gamekeepers and others who raise pheasants hate this gaudy mem-

jay

ber of the crow family (as they do its relations, chick-killers and egg-stealers all). Many a shooting man's hat has some of those blue-barred feathers stuck in its band. But it's not easy to surprise the jay. It's a wary bird. When it does venture out of the trees, it's often to add to its store of food, for the jay is a great dealer in acorns of which it makes a careful cache. It remembers where its larder is – which is more than can be said for one of the mammals of the wood, the grey squirrel.

The grey squirrel likes acorns too, but it buries them in ones and twos all over the shop, and then forgets where it's put them. If you find a little sapling oak growing in an unlikely place, you'll know who planted the acorn that it sprang from.

There's been a lot of criticism of the grey squirrel, some of it rather unfair. It was imported into this country from America just over one hundred years ago, to be released into various private parks, from which of course it soon escaped. Grey squirrels are quick-witted and adaptable, and their numbers soon increased enormously. People said that when it was introduced into this country it drove out the native red squirrel, but that's not strictly true. Disease cut the number of reds drastically, and the greys moved into the gap.

There are still pockets of red squirrels in the British Isles, but usually in remote places. I know of a strangely coloured colony in the Highlands of Scotland. They have red bodies, but pale golden tails and ear-tufts.

On the other hand, the number of grey squirrels is high, and in woodland they are something of a menace, eating many eggs and small birds too. Foresters particularly can't stand them, because the grey squirrels 'ring-bark' their young trees (eat a collar of bark right round the tree, which then dies).

grey squirrel 'ring-barking'

The squirrel comes down to the ground to collect food – pine-cones, beechmast, hazel-nuts and acorns for example – but its safety lies in its tree-climbing skill. When you surprise a squirrel on the ground, watch it climb. It always goes up the far side of the tree from you, keeping out of your sight. But always, if you stand still and watch patiently, curiosity will be too strong for it, and soon you may see a little head peering round the trunk to check on you.

In winter when the trees are bare, a squirrel's 'drey' (that's what its nest is called) is easy to spot.

a squirrel's 'drey'

It's usually about half-way up a tree, say twenty-five to thirty feet high (never below ten feet), and is an untidy mop about a foot across. The outside is made of branches, but it's lined with warmer material like grass, moss, feathers, fur and leaves.

Though the squirrel doesn't hibernate, it certainly takes nice long snoozes inside its drey in the cold weather, only coming out to visit its food stores. If it can remember where they are.

Once I had a large dog that came suddenly upon a small squirrel which was scratching its head and wondering where its larder was. Before I could do anything, the small squirrel vanished into rather a different kind of larder, down the large dog's throat, bushy tail and all.

There are a lot of animals in a wood that are much smaller than the squirrel, such as shrews and voles and wood-mice; but all of them are mostly nocturnal, so that your chances of seeing them are slim.

Even in daytime you'd be lucky to catch sight of a pygmy shrew, because it's so very small, the smallest British mammal. A famous naturalist once weighed two pygmy shrews on a pair of scales, and together they just balanced one old copper ha'penny.

shrew

Shrews have to eat a tremendous amount to keep going, much more than their own weight every day, because their digestions work very quickly, but they themselves are not popular as food for other hunters, because their flesh is musky. Cats will kill them but won't eat them. Owls will, though.

You may find an owl-pellet under a tree, a little ball of hair and bones and claws and teeth, stuff that the owl can't digest and spits out; and often there are shrew skulls in owl-pellets.

You may find other sorts of evidence about unseen animals. If you come upon an old disused bird's nest that, strangely, is full of the skins of

hawthorn berries, that will be a wood-mouse's feeding platform, its dining-table. And if you're very lucky, you might see signs of a dormouse. The dormouse hibernates in winter, falling into so deep a sleep that it is really difficult to wake it; but in summer, it uses ribbons of bark from the honeysuckle to build its nest. Watch out for stripped honeysuckle stems.

You would be very fortunate to see a live dormouse, but there's a good chance you might see a very much larger woodland creature, the badger, if you set about things in the correct way.

43

First, you have to find an occupied badger 'sett' (that's the name for the underground dwelling of a family of badgers). Next, you must find a spot from which you have a good sight of what seem to be the main entrance holes (there may be several). Go out an hour or so before dusk and take up your chosen position, approaching very quietly and carefully, and making sure that any wind is blowing in the right direction – that is, from the sett towards you and not the other way round. Make yourself as comfortable as you can, and keep absolutely still and silent.

Then, with luck, the badgers (again, nocturnal animals) will come out of the sett as the light fades, ready for the night's hunting.

Easy, isn't it? Except that you may have to do this many times before you see a hair of a badger. Patience, patience and yet more patience – that's all you need.

Badgers apart, you'll be amazed how much wildlife you can see, in a wood or anywhere else for that matter, just by the act of sitting perfectly still. Once you are motionless (and a hat pulled down helps to shade your face), animals begin to move. Once you move, they're gone.

The badger is a very large member of the weasel

family. A well-fed adult might weigh thirty pounds or more, and if you should be fortunate enough to get a close view of one, you will see that there is some difference between the sexes. The boars (males) are more heavily built, their heads broader, their tails thinner and whiter. All badgers have a broad white stripe on their faces. This is probably not as a warning to enemies, for badgers have none except man, but as a recognition signal for young cubs.

All badgers have very powerful clawed forefeet for digging, principally, but also for defence, and one of the clues that may lead you to a sett is the finding of a tree, usually an elder, that is scored with long scratch-marks. The badger doesn't do this to sharpen its claws (rather, it would blunt them), but to get mud out from between its toes, and generally because it's a nice stretchy sort of exercise and a way of marking territory at the same time.

You can't mistake a badger sett when you do come upon one. Usually there are a number of entrance holes – a sett that I know of has sixteen – and the regular pathways that the animals beat out on their journeys from home and back again are well-worn and pass under low branches and vegetation (so that you can tell they weren't made

badger sett

by larger animals, like deer). You might find a few hairs on a low fence, black-tipped at each end.

Typically there are four or five large entrances to the sett, and outside each is a mound of excavated earth with bits of old bedding material mixed in it. Underground – out of your sight – are many tunnels, and sleeping and breeding chambers. All these bedrooms need bedding – bracken, hay, straw and grass – which the animals collect and change regularly, sometimes airing it by draping it outside in the sunshine.

Badgers are extremely clean in their habits, and make a dung-pit at some distance from the sett. Often elderberry bushes will grow at this lavatory site, having germinated from pips that the animals have eaten.

The badger walks as the camel does. The two legs on one side go forward, then the two on the other side. It trots, and it gallops when scared or when chasing a rival. However a badger cannot run as fast as a man. I can tell you that, for certain.

One fine summer morning many years ago, I went out early to fetch my cows in for milking. On our farm of those days there was a large field we called the Big Ground (yes, there was also a small field we called the Little Ground, brilliant, eh?), which had recently been mown for hay.

Crossing it was the quickest way to reach the herd, and as I came through the gate I saw, right in the middle of the Big Ground, waddling along over the bluey-green swathes of dewy fresh-cut grass, a low-slung grey shape.

'A badger!' I thought. 'I've never seen a live one really close,' and I ran as hard as I could towards it, hoping to get quite near before it fled. It didn't flee. It didn't take any notice of me when I arrived beside it. It didn't even look at me. Was it deaf? Was it blind? Had it no sense of smell? I felt a fool.

I took off my hat and with it, bending down, I bashed the badger on its bottom.

Nobody would believe (though it's true, I swear it) that for a hundred yards or so I walked slowly along behind a gently snuffling badger, lightly swatting its backside with my hat, till at last we came to a hedge and the animal disappeared through a hole in it, into the woods.

The very next morning I took the very same route, and there, again in the middle of the Big Ground, were two badgers!

'It's my friend,' I thought. 'It's my deaf blind friend with no sense of smell, and *his* friend!' and I galloped happily towards them.

Suddenly, as I drew near, both badgers spun round to face me, and then without hesitation they charged at me side by side, grunting furiously as they came.

If there's one thought worse than having your ankle grabbed by the immensely powerful jaws of a badger, it's having both ankles grabbed by two.

I fled at top speed and proved, thank goodness, that badgers cannot run as fast as a man.

Perhaps because they're not the quickest of movers, a number of badgers are killed on the roads. But then so are a number of foxes, and the fox is very nippy. More likely, I think, both are confused by vehicle headlights and misjudge their crossings. Another possibility is that, ironically, they meet their deaths while scavenging the remains of some other small animal that has already bitten the dust.

At least these deaths are accidental. Drivers do not mean to run over badgers, but some badgers are killed by man quite intentionally, in two principal ways.

The first is by gassing them in their setts. It's thought that badgers may be carriers of the disease bovine tuberculosis, which has been painstakingly eradicated from the dairy herds of this country; and recently, in areas where cattle have once again begun to react to the tuberculin test and where there is also a large badger population, systematic gassing has been carried out. Whether or not this is a right decision – and I'm not at all sure that it is – at least it is done as humanely as possible, and for a reason.

What is done for no good reason, without mercy, and in the name of 'sport', is both badger-digging and badger-baiting, as horrid and unsporting pursuits as you can imagine, and both illegal. Man is not only the most intelligent of the world's animals. He can also be the cruellest, and even in this day and age, there are badgers who have to face this cruelty.

I won't go into details, because the whole thing makes me feel sick, but there are men who send terriers down a sett to fight the badger and keep it occupied while they dig down to it, till at last a smashing blow on its skull with the flat of a spade puts it out of its misery.

In badger-baiting, that misery is prolonged. When the sportsmen have dug down far enough to reach the animal, they pick it up with a great pair of tongs and drop it into a stout sack. Then later they turn it out into a pit or other enclosure, to fight a number of dogs. The badger's a brave fighter, and the bite of its strong jaws can cripple many a dog, but there's only one end for it at last, and it's a hard and terrible death.

Sometimes the diggers come upon a sow badger

with cubs, and it may happen that a cub is spared that whack on the head and is reared as a pet. Here's the true story of such a one.

My brother had always wanted a pet badger, and one day a gamekeeper friend told him of a cub, sole survivor of a dig. It was a little sow, remarkable for having an unusually wide white stripe down her face. My brother reared her on a bottle.

He called her Wilhelmina, and she grew up as tame as could be, playing happily with his terriers as though she were a dog herself. When he came home from work, Wilhelmina would squeak with joy and nip his legs in her own special way of greeting. She learned to walk on a collar and lead, and liked to go into the pub for a drink of beer.

At last, when Wilhelmina was full-grown, the call of the wild proved too strong for her, and one night she chewed her way out of the little shed that was her home, and was gone.

My brother only saw her once again.

Two years had passed, and he was driving home one winter's evening when a badger stepped out into the lane so suddenly that he had no chance to brake. He hit it, and killed it. It was a sow badger. She had an unusually wide white stripe down her face.

Many English men and women have a special relationship with another of the larger woodland animals, the fox. They hunt it.

A great deal of nonsense is talked about the rights and wrongs of fox-hunting. Those who support it say that foxes must be controlled (because they kill poultry) and that hunting them with a pack of hounds is the only proper and efficient way to do it; the loonier ones claim that the fox actually enjoys the sport. Those who are against it see fox-hunting folk as terribly cruel and bloodthirsty, which most of them aren't, particularly.

For hundreds of years fox-hunting with all its pageantry has been a part of the English country scene, and part of English poetry and story, painting and song. Despite all that, I happen to think that it should be stopped, for the simplest of reasons. It's not fair to the fox.

To begin with, I don't believe that he does all that much damage. If you forget to shut your chickens up at night, more fool you. He'll kill them. He'll probably kill them all, because instinctively as long as something flutters in front of him, he'll snap at it. And of course the fox will sometimes take poultry by day.

fox

The duck that's waddled too far from the pond, the broody hen that's chosen to make a nest in the hedge-bottom, the cockerels that have ranged too far – all are fair game.

One April day a fox killed sixteen of my cockerels in a few moments, and when I got up to milk the following morning, and pulled back the curtains and looked out of the bedroom window, there he was, sitting on the lawn below beside the sundial, looking up at me, ears cocked. His red coat shone, his front paws were neatly together, his white-tipped brush was curled around him.

I dressed quickly and ran downstairs for my gun. I didn't know if this was the cockerel-killer or not, but I didn't care. He was going to pay for the massacre.

When I peeped over the garden wall, there was no sign of the fox. Well, that's not quite true – there was one. Fox-droppings are called 'scats'. He had left a present for me, a nice steaming pile of them on the steps of the sundial. Yes, I would have shot him, but still I don't think that anything a fox does ought to condemn him to a long terrifying chase and an exhausted bitter death in the jaws of a pack of hounds.

There is such a thing as a drag-hunt. A bag of artificial scent is dragged across country, and hounds can run happily after that trail, and hunting folk can gallop happily after them and jump over hedges and fences, and everything will seem to be just as it should – the music of hounds, the beautiful horses, the humans dressed fit to kill. Except that they won't kill anything. And that, however the followers dress up their arguments, is why drag-hunting will never catch on and fox-hunting will never stop, until it's banned by law. Blood sports are about killing things, and if there's no blood, says the foxhunter, there's no sport.

Console yourself by knowing that far more foxes get away than are killed, because the fox, unlike for example the hare, is a highly intelligent animal, and a great hunter in his own right.

Rabbit, hare, squirrel, vole, mouse, hedgehog – all fall victim to the fox, as do pheasants and partridges and snails and beetles and loads of earthworms. And the fox is a survivor in hard times too, eating carrion, and if needs be keeping going on berries and other fruit.

Except at the breeding season, the fox is a solitary animal, and a mainly nocturnal one too, spending the day in his 'earth'. This is often an old rabbit burrow (he'll have eaten the owners), or part of a badger sett where he will take a room and mark it with his strong-smelling scent glands. The cleanly badgers turn up their noses in disgust at this stinking lodger, but they put up with him nevertheless. I know of one sett that houses badger, fox and rabbit, strange though that seems.

Around January, you may hear in the woods the weird scream of the vixen, the female, as she seeks a mate, and the cubs, usually around four, are born about April. The dog-fox helps in their upbringing

vixen with cubs

by carrying food to the earth; and the vixen stays with her cubs, teaching them to hunt and to avoid the dangers that threaten them, till the autumn, when the family group breaks up.

Then the young foxes must go their own way, and soon the sound of the horn is heard again in the woods and the eager whimper of hounds, for now cub-hunting begins. Some of those cubs will not live to hear the coming of the cuckoo next spring.

The cuckoo is the idlest of all woodland birds, of all birds, I should think. The female does no nest-making, no brooding and hatching, and has no duties as a mother. She simply drops an egg in someone else's nest, usually that of a dunnock or a meadow pipit or a reed warbler. She may lay ten or a dozen eggs, each in a different nest. When it hatches, the baby cuckoo, far bigger than its nest-mates, turns its back on them and with strong heaves, tips each in turn out of the nest to die on the ground below. Now it has all the food the anxious foster-parents can bring.

cuckoo

It's the male cuckoo who cries his name – the female makes a bubbling noise – and both are very fond of the woolly caterpillars of moths. At the end of a nice easy summer, off they go on holiday to Africa for some more sunshine. There are lots of rhymes about the cuckoo's stay with us. Here's one:

> In April, come he will.
> In May, he sings all day.
> In June, he changes his tune.
> In July, away he'll fly.
> In August, go he must.

For me the sound of the first cuckoo each year, like the sight of the first returning swallow, is always very exciting.

But there's one other summer visitor from Africa who must be the greatest songster of all, the nightingale. Despite its name it sings just as much by day (you notice the song more at night because everything's quiet). And what a song it is, of deep full notes and trills and warbles. It's a shy bird, this little brown thrush, and you may not catch sight of it, but if you are lucky enough to have one visit your wood, hearing it is the greatest treat.

There is room in the woods for a whole lot of other birds, the flycatcher, the nuthatch, the tree-creeper and many more, but no room in this book for all of them. I'm just picking two more, both to me typical woodland birds. One is of the day, one of the night.

The first is the pheasant. Pheasants came originally from China, probably brought here by the Romans, and the cock birds are very colourful and showy, with bright-red featherless faces. On their heads are two sprouts of feathers called 'ear-tufts', and the body colour is a handsome mixture of cream and black and green and purple on a chestnut background, ending in a very long tail. In springtime the cock pheasants are very noisy in the woods, crying 'Cok-cok-cok!' and ruffling their feathers and flapping their wings as they crow, like domestic cockerels. The hen birds are brown and quiet.

If you come upon a pheasant suddenly, it will rocket up out of the undergrowth with a tremendous clatter, as it does before the beaters who walk through the wood beating the bushes and trees with sticks to drive the birds up before the guns (another blood sport but at least, unlike fox-hunting, this is killing something that can be eaten).

hen and cock pheasant

But pheasants are normally shy by nature, and you are more likely to see them run, head down, to hide rather than fly. Most probably, in fact, you'll catch sight of them when they come out of the woods to forage in the open fields.

The night bird that for me is the very spirit of the woods is the tawny owl. You may not set eyes on him but you can't fail to hear him.

You might just see him by day if you follow the sound of angry squeaking and chittering from a host of little birds – robins, tits and finches – who have come upon him as he sits motionless beside

his tree-hole. They are mobbing him, shouting rude things at him, but he takes no notice. His hunting time – for some of those small birds, for rats and mice and young rabbits and beetles – is in the hours of darkness, when that long eerie call wavers through the trees. 'Tu-whit, tu-whoo!' is what you think he says, but in fact what you hear is one bird saying 'Ker-wick!' and its mate answering, 'Hooo-hoo-oo!'

Last, before we leave the woods there are the deer, once the pride of the forests that covered most of England. Deer, the King's beasts, that common folk had no right to hunt.

The largest, the red deer, is now found mainly on Exmoor or in the Highlands of Scotland (we'll be hearing more about them in Chapter 5), and the middle-sized fallow deer are often in fenced deer-parks, but there are plenty of both in places like the New Forest.

The last of the three commonest kinds of British deer is the roe, a much smaller animal that lives in little family groups in woods and conifer planta-tions. With roe deer, as with fallow deer, the males are called bucks, the females does, and the young ones fawns. The buck's antlers are not large, and its coat is brown in summer but longer and greyish in winter. The fawns are spotted (but very hard to spot). Whenever the doe leaves them both (almost always she has twins) to go and forage, they lie absolutely motionless, relying on stillness and camouflage. You could almost step on one, yet never see it, though you might hear what sounds like a little dog barking, which is the mother's alarm call. At dawn and dusk roe deer will come out of the woods to graze in nearby fields, and indeed sometimes in nearby gardens where they can do a lot of damage. They have a special liking

roe deer (buck, left; doe, centre; fawns, foreground)

for rose-petals – any colour – which doesn't exactly make them popular with growers.

Not long ago I had a great thrill as I sat in my hide, pipe in mouth, pen in hand, staring dreamily out across Burr Acre.

Suddenly, there was a single adult roe, bounding stiff-legged across the field! For a moment I lost sight of it behind hedgerow trees, and then saw it again, through my binoculars, in the next field. It was flustered, leaping here and there, and for perhaps half a minute I had a splendid view of the little deer. It was quite the most exciting thing I've ever seen from the window of my hide. So far. At last it made off, bouncing away till it was lost to my sight.

I don't know why it was out in open country in broad daylight, at least a couple of miles as the roe runs from the nearest piece of woodland. Maybe it had been chased by dogs, and in escaping had lost its bearings. I just kept my fingers crossed that it would get safely over the road and back to the shelter and security of the woods.

Chapter 4

IN THE HEDGEROWS

A hedge, you could say, is a kind of very long, thin, miniature wood. Like a wood it offers food and shelter and concealment. Many of the animals that use hedges, at the boundaries of fields or at the sides of roads and lanes, also live in woods; but you may see them more easily in and around the hedgerows.

One that gets its name from its habit of hunting noisily along the hedge-bottoms and the sides of ditches, is the hedgehog.

If you've never met a live one, you've probably seen a dead hedgehog – on the roads, where many are killed. The five thousand needle-sharp spines, that protect them as they curl up before the threat of a predator, are no use against a car or a lorry.

Hedgehogs are mainly nocturnal, and they make a lot of noise as they forage for worms and slugs and beetles, specially when they're crunching snails. They have to do a lot of eating between April and October, to store enough fat to last them till the following spring, because they hibernate through the winter. This is the time when most die, particularly young ones born late in the year who haven't had enough time to build up a fat reserve.

Last summer I was driving down our lane, and there was a full-grown hedgehog standing in the middle of the road, just asking to be run over. I stopped and picked it up (with a thick cloth) and took it home. It didn't seem to have been injured or be ill, but just in case, I kept it in a rabbit hutch and fed it on worms and snails and a hedgehog's favourite food, tinned dog-meat. There was no knowing if it was a boar or a sow, so we called it Leslie. There was certainly nothing wrong with Leslie's appetite, so after a few days we let him/her go into the garden to find his/her own food, but he/she disappeared without so much as a 'Thank you'.

There was another hedgehog that we found a long time ago, at night, in the same sort of way. As

hedgehog

we drove home, there was one sitting in the glare of the headlights, right in the middle of the farm gateway. So we picked it up. But this time there was no doubt about its sex.

Next morning we looked into the hutch where we'd put it, and there were five hedgehogs. The four babies were droopy-eared, blind and pink, each with a few pale rubbery spines.

We had two choices, to take mother and children and put them in a dry hedge-bottom and hope for the best, or – which seemed more sensible – to leave well alone, so that we could feed the sow and keep an eye on things.

The idea of rearing four baby hedgehogs was an attractive one, so we left the family in the hutch; but it was the wrong choice. Probably from the shock of having been 'rescued' just when she was searching for a suitable place to give birth, the sow did not feed the babies, would not go near them, and they all died.

Hedgerows provide a good home for many birds and for a lot of rodents – rats and mice and voles. And all of these provide good hunting for a couple of fierce little beasts, the weasel and the stoat.

The weasel family is an odd one. In this country there are two rare ones, the pine marten and the polecat; two big ones, the badger and the otter; and one small one, the stoat; and one very small one, the weasel itself.

The weasel is a bloodthirsty fellow, and will kill full-grown rabbits and rats three times its own weight. These victims often seemed paralysed by sheer terror at the approach of stoat or weasel, and will wait, squealing, till a bite under the jaw ends it all.

Weasels work mainly at night, hunting the verges and ditches and climbing in the hedges after birds, their babies and their eggs. But you may see one by day crossing a lane or path in front of you. Its body is so long and its legs so short that it seems

weasel

to glide across like a red-brown ripple, very fast and low.

The stoat is more than a foot long, much bigger than the tiny weasel, and has a black-tipped tail and more obvious yellowy-white on its belly. It

70

is a great killer, of the farmer's hens or the game-keeper's young pheasants, and sometimes it will hunt in small packs of family groups.

There have always been stories – rather scary stories – of a person walking alone, along a bridle path perhaps, when suddenly he hears rustlings in the bordering hedges and the sound of thin, snick-ering, snarling, yakkering voices. All of a sudden little faces pop up, first one, then another, then ten or a dozen, wicked-looking little triangular faces all staring at the man, and he turns, and runs. For his life perhaps?

Stories like that always give me a small cold shiver when I meet a stoat, as I did the other morning, walking early with Sam the German Shepherd. The stoat came out of the laneside grass twenty or thirty yards ahead, and looked at me, head cocked, one paw raised, black-tipped tail twitching, before diving back into cover. The dog was busy with an interesting smell in the ditch and didn't see the stoat pop out twice more and stare at us (or were there three stoats, I thought, and more to come?).

We walked on, and Sam caught the scent and began to rootle about in the grass tufts, but the stoat (or stoats?) had vanished down some handy hole, perhaps a vole's run.

Two hedgerow residents preyed upon by stoats

and weasels are the bank vole and the long-tailed fieldmouse.

Voles look different from other members of the mouse family; stumpier, stockier, with blunt heads and short round ears and a stiff little tail. The bank

vole

vole is bright red, and makes shallow runs in roadside banks or under hedges, and climbs among branches after berries, seeds and nuts.

The fieldmouse, much smaller, with large dark eyes for it is mainly nocturnal, is also very fond of nuts, and you can play detective if you come across nut shells in a hedgerow. The vole holds the nut away from itself and opens it neatly, leaving a

tidily gnawed rim that shows no teeth marks on the outer surface. If you find a nut with teethmarks on the outside of the shell, that's the work of a fieldmouse. Squirrels, that have much more powerful incisor teeth, split the hazel-nut in two, and birds just leave jagged broken holes in it.

There are umpteen sorts of birds that you might see in a hedge but, just as we started the wayside mammals with the hedgehog, let's begin with the hedge-sparrow. And the first thing to be said, is that it's not a sparrow at all, no relation to the

dunnock

house-sparrow and the tree-sparrow. Its proper
name is the dunnock. It's a quiet little brown bird
with a slaty-blue breast, and it creeps about, on the
ground mainly, in a mouselike way. It has the thin
bill of an insect-eater (seed-eaters have a shorter,
stouter beak), and sings a sweet clear 'sweedle-
deedle-deedle' song, rather like the wren's.

What you notice about the wren's song is how
loud it is. You don't expect such a volume of sound
from one of our smallest birds.

It's a very clear sweet song, full of happy trills,
but the wren also makes a couple of other noises – a
sharp 'stit-stit' if he's rather angry with you for

coming near his territory, and a very loud, stroppy 'chur-r-r!' when he's really annoyed.

Although you may see him creeping about among the branches, again, like a mouse, there's nothing mousy about the wren. He's a very bossy, self-important fellow, and in fable he appears as the King of the Birds. The French name for him actually is '*le roi des oiseaux*'.

You can't mistake this little brown bird. Flying, he whizzes about like an oversized bumble bee. Sitting, he will bob angrily up and down at you, his little tail cocked right up.

The cock bird builds a nest, often in a hole in a wall (one used to build under the eaves of my

wren

garden shed), and a very beautiful nest it is. He makes it out of moss, leaves, grass and wool, and it is domed, a globe, with an entrance hole in one side. The trouble is that the hen is very choosy, and so the cock has to build several nests till he's made one that she thinks is just right. This one she will line with feathers, and then he can heave a sigh of relief and stop work.

Every animal has a Latin name, and the little wren has a big one – *Troglodytes Troglodytes Troglodytes*! Because a troglodyte is someone who lives in a cave, a dark, safe, dry place with just a small hole to enter. In the bitterest winter weather, large numbers of these little cave-dwellers will huddle together for warmth. Amazingly, in the terrible winter of 1962–3, a nest-box put up for tits was found to contain fifty wrens.

A family of birds that are commonly seen in hedgerows and by waysides are the finches, especially the chaffinch with his slaty-blue head and pink breast (the hen, as so often in birds, is duller). If you don't see the chaffinch, you're certain to hear it in springtime, when it sings its special song over and over again, all day long. The song has about twelve notes and ends with an upward flourish – 'choo-ee-o!'

Perhaps because the cock chaffinch always seems to be singing alone, his Latin name is *Coelebs*, which means 'bachelor', but that's not true – he's a happily married bird.

The bullfinch is very handsome, stockier than the chaffinch, with a dramatic rose-pink breast, black head and blue-grey back. Its beak too is stouter and the bullfinch uses it to eat, among other things, the buds of fruit trees. It is said that one bullfinch eats 12,000 buds in a year, though how on earth anyone works that out, I don't know. But you can see why it's not popular with fruit-growers.

If there are thistles by the roadside, you may see goldfinches flittering about with their special dancing flight, for thistle-seeds are a favourite food. A flock of goldfinches is called a 'charm', and very charming little birds they are, with brilliant scarlet, black and white heads, and black-and-yellow wings. Their song is a liquid twitter, a bit like a canary's but higher and more tinkly, and, perhaps because of it, thousands of wild goldfinches used to be caught and sold as cage-birds (as did bullfinches). Wild creatures do not take kindly to captivity and most of these prisoners died, before sale or soon after. So it's a mercy that it is now against the law to catch them.

One other bird that you're sure to see, perching on the hedge-top and keeping always just ahead of you as you walk, is the yellowhammer. It is a bunting, another sort of finch, and you can't mistake its bright lemon-yellow head. You can't mistake its song either. 'Chi-chi-chi-chi-chi—chwee!' it sings, or, in our language 'A-little-bit-of-bread-and-no-cheese!'

yellowhammer

bullfinch

People have always liked to put words to birdsong, like the woodpigeon's 'Tak' two coos, Taffy, tak' two'. And next time you hear a song-thrush, you can choose between four versions. 'Summer's coming, summer's coming, I know it, I know it!', 'Did he do it? Did he do it? Come out! Come out!', 'How d'ye do? Bo-Peep, Bo-Peep!' and (my favourite), 'Judy! Judy! Pretty Dick!'.

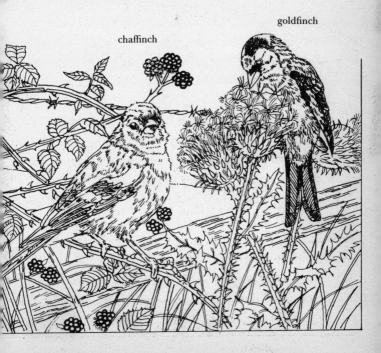

chaffinch

goldfinch

In winter you won't hear an awful lot of song, for birds are too busy foraging for food to keep alive, but when the early light arrives, in spring, the cock birds' thoughts turn to owning a territory and a mate. Each chooses a high perch – a tree or an artificial tree like a telegraph post – to get the best view and reach the biggest possible audience. And so we hear the 'dawn chorus', each song proclaiming a different species.

And there are so many species that you might come across at the side of the road or lane, not just of mammals and birds, but of butterflies and bees and beetles, of slugs and snails and spiders – far too many to mention here. But before we leave the hedgerow, here's a little experiment you can try. Nothing to do with animals, but rather fun all the same.

You can tell the age of a hedge. Like this.

Pace out thirty strides along one side of a hedge and as you go along count how many different sorts of trees and shrubs you see in that distance (for example – ash, hedge maple, elder, hawthorn, dog-rose). Disregard ivy, brambles and climbers. Then multiply your total by one hundred, and you'll know (roughly) how old that hedge is.

Just suppose you counted as many as ten varieties in those thirty strides. That hedge must have been planted by the Saxons! A thousand years ago, the King of the Birds would have peeped out of it, swearing angrily at a passing Saxon farmer.

Chapter 5

ON MOOR AND MOUNTAINS

Although none of them are terribly high, there are mountains in England and Wales, but whenever I think of mountains, I think of the Highlands of Scotland. And when I think of the Highlands, I think of the largest wild animal of the British Isles, the red deer.

Of course there are nowhere near as many red deer now as when our country was thickly forested, but in the Highlands there are still about 190,000. Although some people are allowed (wrongly, I think) to shoot them for sport, that's all very carefully controlled by law, so that only a certain number may be killed.

Nowadays there are quite a few commercial deer

farms, where the animals are bred and reared for their meat. Deer meat is called venison. It fetches a good price (which I'm afraid attracts poachers who often use cruel methods of killing), and it's very tasty, as Robin Hood and his merrie men, greatest of poachers, well knew.

For myself, I like to eat most kinds of meat. I just hope that the animal that provided it did not suffer unduly, at its death or before it. But more and more people are beginning to question whether it is right for us to sentence other creatures to death, for food (especially perhaps very young ones, like calves for veal). If you feel strongly about this, then you can do something about it. You can become a vegetarian. That's your choice.

The red deer is of course naturally a vegetarian, eating herbage and the young shoots of trees and shrubs. Although we may think of them as creatures of moor and mountain, red deer are woodlanders by nature, and the damage they can do doesn't endear them to the forester, or to the farmer, when they break into his wheatfields. A herd of deer can ruin a whole field of turnips or potatoes in a night.

The males are called stags, the females hinds, and the young ones calves (unlike the terms for fallow and roe deer, which we met in Chapter 3), but the great stags are the ones that catch the eye. The red deer hinds are hornless, but the stag grows antlers that increase in size each year of the beast's life. They don't just stay there and get bigger like a tree. Early each April every stag loses his antlers. The blood supply to them stops and they drop off. You may well pick up a single antler in the heather. I've got one that I use in the garden for scratching out drills for small seeds.

Then, through the summer, the new antlers grow, fed by a soft grey covering – a mass of tiny blood-vessels called 'velvet'. In August the stag rubs off the velvet by bashing its antlers against bushes, and then the new clean ones are ready for the fights of the mating season, called the 'rut'.

The rut takes place in the first half of October, when the glens are filled with the weird noise of the stags roaring as they challenge one another for possession of a group of hinds. It's called 'belling', this noise, and it's a kind of cross between the bellow of a bull and the roar of a lion.

I remember once, in Scotland, we were walking with one of our dogs, Dodo, during the rut, and the noise of stags was all around us. We came over a little rise in the ground, and there, not a dozen yards away, was a huge stag, eyes blazing, muzzle thrust forward so that his great spread of antlers lay back against his shaggy mane as he roared defiance at a rival. It was foolish of us to have taken such a risk. That walk might have had a very nasty ending.

You can tell the age of a red deer stag by the development of the antlers. A second-year male (called a 'pricket') just has two knobs. In the third year, the 'brow', the first branching point, is added either side, and then more points are added with each year's growth of new horns. By about the age of six, the stag should have 'brow', 'bay', and 'trey', with probably a couple of points called 'two a'top' at the extremity of each antler. Incidentally, the brow, bay and trey together are called the 'rights'.

Then the number of points a'top increases each year till a stag in his prime, at ten or twelve years old, could possibly have a head like this: brow, bay and trey and perhaps four a'top on one side and five a'top the other, making him a 15-pointer. Anything with a head of over twelve points is called a 'royal', and it is these big heads that the deerstalkers look for.

Hopefully it's a clean kill (not always the case, I fear), and then in due course that proud head will hang upon some wall beneath its crowning

red deer (stag in foreground) and golden eagle

glory, staring down upon its killer with eyes of glass.

Higher still, above the red deer of the Highlands, the keenest of eyes are searching the ground far below. They belong to the largest bird of prey that we have – the golden eagle with its six-foot wing-span.

You can think yourself very lucky if you catch sight of this magnificent creature (I never have), but on a moorland walk you may well see the bird that it preys on, the red grouse. Golden eagles have always been persecuted for taking grouse. And why? Because another more powerful and more ruthless animal, man, also wants the grouse for food. The sport of grouse-shooting might well have led to the extinction of the golden eagle, but happily its numbers are now on the increase.

It's odd to think of a bird as an important grazing animal but that's what the red grouse is. The grouse eats the young green shoots of the heather, that plant which covers so much of moorland, but it also needs the cover of the older and woodier bushes.

So as to make sure of providing both, grouse moors are burned regularly, usually in patches of an acre or so about every ten years. This burning

red grouse

('swaling', it's called in the North, 'muirburn' in Scotland) ensures plenty of new young growth from the heather.

One thing you have to say for shooting-men – some good comes from their activities. In the lowlands, many small woods are kept (for the sake of the pheasant) that might otherwise be cut down; and if there was no grouse-shooting on the uplands, the grouse-moors might well be covered with yet more of those great, dark, soulless plantations of conifers.

'Go back! Go back! Go back!' cries the red grouse as it flies low over the roll of the ground with rapid wing-beats and long glides. Whether its message is to other grouse or to the men with guns is anyone's guess.

In areas like North Wales and the Lake District there are herds of wild goats on the hills and mountains. They are the descendants of domestic animals that have escaped, and without any particular enemies (the last British wolf, for example, was killed in 1743) they have thrived.

wild mountain goats

About twenty years ago a cousin of mine turned a billy and a couple of nanny goats loose in a high rocky valley. Recently I met a man who had visited this part of Exmoor, and we were talking about animals. He told me of the large herd of wild goats, long-horned, shaggy and multi-coloured, that he had seen there leaping sure-footedly among the boulders.

'Of course,' he said knowledgeably, 'they've been there many hundreds of years, you know.'

'Oh yes?' I said. Oh no, I thought, they haven't. It's just that Cousin Nell's goats have had an awful lot of kids.

When an animal of the uplands dies, there are always scavengers at hand to clear up the body. One of these is the hooded crow, the 'hoodie' as the

hooded crow

Scots call it for it doesn't appear further south. The hoodie is the same size as the carrion crow but easy to distinguish, because although head, wings and tail are black, its back and underparts are grey.

But if one of my cousin's goats breathes its last

on Exmoor, two likely scavengers are the raven and the buzzard.

If you're walking on moor or mountain and hear the deepest of croaks (it sounds like 'Pruk! Pruk!'), and see high above a bulky black bird with a wedge-shaped tail and a heavy bill above a shaggy throat, that is the raven, greatest of the crows. You might be very lucky and see a pair of ravens on their courting flight, complete with acrobatic rolls and lunges. Or, because the raven has the crow family's love of mischief, you could see them teasing and taunting another large bird of the moorland, the buzzard; they dive at it in a series of near-misses, or roll over on their backs beneath it and stab upwards with those great beaks, while the big hawk flaps desperately and gives its melancholy cry 'Mee-oo!'

Usually the buzzard soars for hours with hardly a beat of its wings, broad and blunt, like the wings of a giant moth. Often you may see it perched motionless on top of a roadside telegraph pole. Though both raven and buzzard are carrion-eaters, each feeds also on live prey – small animals and birds, and, in the case of the raven, eggs, grubs, grain and fruit, while the buzzard will catch reptiles like lizards and snakes.

On one exciting occasion I actually saw a

buzzard

buzzard from the window of my hide. The nearest moorland is many miles distant from my house, but there are a few pairs of buzzards that breed regularly in a wood on the nearby hills.

Just think for a moment of the hills of Britain, of the hills, the moorland, the mountains. There is one kind of animal that you'll find up there in its millions – far, far more than any other that we've talked about – grazing away, right up to the very mountain tops, and you find them all over the lowlands as well. Just at the moment there are sixteen and a half million of them in England and

Wales and heaven knows how many more in Scotland, where you can't move an inch without meeting one. You haven't guessed? I'll give you a hint. These animals are not wild.

Chapter 6

ON THE FARM

The answer is – sheep. While you're keeping your eyes skinned for wild animals, you're bound to see many, many more tame ones, animals that have been domesticated for man's use.

There came a time, thousands of years ago, when early man realized that instead of just hunting animals to kill them for food, he could make much better use of them if he kept them alive. By doing this he could breed as many as he liked of each kind, to produce milk and meat and hides and fleeces, and to pull heavy weights for him. So instead of roaming from one hunting ground to another, he began to acquire flocks and herds to keep them in one place where he could settle down and stay. In fact, he became a farmer.

The sheep is one of the most useful of man's tamed animals. To begin with, it's a very good grazer in two ways.

On good pastures, the sheep crops the herbage very close to the ground, and this controls weeds and encourages new growth of grass; also, being a lightweight, in wet weather it does not 'poach' the land (tread it into a muddy squidge, as cattle would). In addition, its dung makes excellent manure.

On rough land where the grazing is poor, sheep will still make the best of it, and on steep hills and mountain slopes that are of no use to cattle they can live and thrive, even in hard weather.

To protect them from the cold of winter, sheep grow a thick coat that we call a fleece, and the wool from this coat is used to make all kinds of clothing. Farmers don't have to kill the sheep to get its coat. They simply shear it off, usually about June (a skilled shearer can clip as many as 200 in a day), and then the animal is comfortable in light summer woollies. Before the following winter it will once again have grown a warm fleece. As well as providing wool, in some parts of the world sheep are kept for their milk, and in this country there are a number of flocks of milking ewes. The milk is excellent for cheese-making.

But the chief value of sheep is as a source of what most of us eat a lot of (often too much) – meat. The meat of the adult animal (called mutton) used to be widely eaten, but nowadays it's not much in fashion. Today's popular sheep-meat is lamb.

That doesn't mean that we eat those pretty little creatures that we see frisking and gambolling about the fields in the early spring. Who could possibly kill such delightful babies? Oh no, we wait till they're nice and fat, about four months old, say, and weigh about eighty pounds.

Many ewes have twins, and so the sheep farmer has a big crop of lambs to sell by the end of the season. Some females will be reared on, to replace older ewes in the flock, but most of them, and almost all the male lambs (for only one ram needs to be kept to mate with sixty or more ewes) will go to the butcher.

Because the sheep is such a useful beast, there aren't many parts of the countryside where you won't see a flock. But next time you do, don't just think 'Ah – sheep.' That's almost as boring a way of looking at animals as seeing something flying, and thinking 'Ah – a bird.' The point is – what bird

is it? It doesn't have to be a tremendously rare one – that's not what this book's about. There's so much that's interesting about perfectly ordinary animals if you really focus on them and think about them.

Just as it's worth being able to tell a crow from a rook, so it's fun to try to recognize what breed of sheep you're seeing. It's a good game to play on a long car journey (provided the driver keeps his eyes on the road), or from the window of a train, for there are forty-eight different breeds of sheep in Britain alone.

Here are just a dozen that you might see.

In upland country there is the Welsh Mountain and the Blackface, the Dartmoor – a big heavy animal, and the Cheviot – a small neat beast with a very white face. Both sexes of the Blackface and the rams of the Welsh Mountain have curling horns, and if you see little whitish blobs right up on the mountain-tops in Scotland or Wales, they'll

Dartmoor

Welsh Mountain   Romney Marsh

probably be sheep of one or other of these types.
Then there are long-woolled varieties, like the
Romney Marsh, the Leicester, the Lincoln and the
Devon, and short-woolled sheep like the South-
downs, the Hampshire Down with its black nose,
the Suffolk, a big rangy sheep with an all-black
head and a Roman nose that gives it a solemn,
almost sad expression, and the Dorset Horn that
has the longest, curliest horns of all. Often you may
see a flock in October and November, when the

Devon

Dorset Horn

Suffolk

rams are turned in with the ewes, and notice that the ewes are of one breed and the rams of quite a different one. The lambs that are born the following spring will be cross-bred; a good idea, because cross-breeding produces animals that are strong and fatten well.

There's an uncommon breed that you're quite likely to spot (and that's the right word, because these sheep are spotted with big blotches of black

Jacob's sheep

or dark brown). They are Jacob's Sheep, so called from the Bible story of the time when Jacob worked as a shepherd for his father-in-law. He was paid in kind, by being allowed to keep all the spotted sheep born in the flock. Maybe it was from their fleeces that the coat of many colours was made for Jacob's favourite son, Joseph. A strange thing about this woolly, long-tailed variety is that, while some have only two horns, many have four, and sometimes even six!

There are probably about 4,000 Jacob's Sheep in the country, so you've got a good chance of coming across some. And there are other, rarer sheep, that you might just be lucky enough to see.

These are the primitive breeds, dark-fleeced and small and quick, living examples of the first sheep that man domesticated. Mostly they're in private parks or zoos, but one sort that you might meet is the Soay sheep.

'Soay' is a Viking word that means 'Sheep Isle', which is what the Norsemen named one Scottish island that they discovered, with its population of little brown sheep. Soay sheep actually shed their coarse hair-like wool in summer, so their owners have no need to shear them. They simply pluck them. Shetland sheep are another primitive kind that are plucked, or 'rued' as it's called, rather than being shorn.

I've tried my hand at ruing, and the wool comes off very easily and it doesn't hurt the animal at all.

I've never done any shearing, though – I'm clumsy, and I'm sure I'd make an awful mess of the sheep – but I've helped at shearing-time, catching up animals for the shearers and rolling up the thick, smelly, greasy fleeces afterwards.

In fact I've never actually kept sheep, because when we were farming a public footpath ran right across the land, and people who walked on it did not always have their dogs under control. Always remember, if you have a dog, to keep it firmly under control in the countryside, especially near sheep. If a farmer catches a dog in the act of worrying sheep, he has a perfect right to shoot it.

The animals that I kept when I was a farmer were dairy cows, and though there aren't as many of them about as sheep, there are plenty about the place – two and a quarter million at the last count.

Sadly, eight out of every ten of that two and a quarter million are black-and-white – British Friesians. I've nothing against the British Friesian cow, a marvellous animal that produces ninety per cent of the milk in this country and sixty per cent of the beef as well. I'm only sad that because there are so many of them, there are now comparatively so few of the other breeds so common fifty years and more ago.

You can't blame the dairy farmer for choosing the most efficient kind of cow. I did it myself, starting out with a herd of many colours, and ending up with nothing but black-and-whites. It's just a pity that, because Friesians are such efficient converters of the food they eat into the milk and meat that we want, other varieties have become scarce, and sometimes nearly extinct. But there are, thankfully, still enough left of the more important dairy and beef breeds to make cattle-spotting interesting.

The four dairy breeds you're most likely to see are the Ayrshire, the Shorthorn, the Jersey and the Guernsey.

Ayrshires are lighter and neater than the big Friesian. Depending on how you look at it, the Friesian gives the impression of being a black beast with white patches, or a white beast with black patches. I once had a whitish Friesian with an almost perfect black map of Africa on her side.

The Ayrshire's colour patches, of red or brown or, occasionally, black, are scattered about on a white background in a spottier, more broken, fashion. In its natural state, the Ayrshire has large, wide-set, upward-curving horns. But you're un-likely to see them, because most calves (of all breeds) are de-horned at a very young age and so remain 'polled' or hornless, a sensible step which saves a lot of damage and injury.

There are still a good many pure-bred Ayrshire herds about, but not as many Shorthorns. More's the pity, since a herd of Shorthorns is always a nice sight on account of the variety of colours in the breed. Some are bright red, some pure white, some red-and-white, and many are different shades of roan which is a blend between these two colours. My favourite is strawberry roan, a very attractive reddish mixture. Again, Shorthorns today don't usually live up to their name. They're mostly No-horns, and the same applies to the other two well-known dairy breeds, the Jersey and the Guernsey.

Both these – you won't be surprised to hear – came originally from the Channel Islands, and both give particularly rich milk.

The Guernsey is the larger of the two, often called the Golden Guernsey, as much for the col-our of its milk as for its coat, which is a fine yellowy-fawn, with or without white markings. The head is long and narrow, the eyes large and gentle, the nostrils wide.

The Jersey is noticeably smaller, and its coat colour varies more, ranging from fawn to brown or brownish-black, either whole or broken up with white patches, and the head of the Jersey is unmistakable. It's a short head, with a dark muzzle

Jersey cow and calf

surrounded by a ring of light-coloured hair, and its face is 'dished' or concave between the eyes. Elegant and fine-boned, the Jersey has a deer-like look, and the cows are very docile and quiet. In complete contrast, Jersey bulls are fiery and quick and not to be trusted an inch.

Two popular breeds of beef cattle are the Aberdeen Angus and the Hereford. The Angus has an all-black silky coat, and is a very deep-bodied, short-legged animal. If you see a black beast with horns, then it's definitely not an Angus, because they are naturally polled.

Angus bulls are used for mating with heifers of other breeds, because the calves born of this cross are small, resulting in easier birth. (By the way, a female animal is called a heifer until it drops its second calf. Then it graduates to being a cow.)

Both Angus and Hereford bulls are reasonably placid as a rule, and the Hereford bull is also much used as an 'outlier', running free with the herd rather than being kept in a bull-pen as the more dangerous dairy bulls are.

You can't miss the Hereford. It has a red body and an all-white face, and that white face is transmitted to all its calves, regardless of the breed of the mother. It's very common to see black animals with white faces, and these fattening beasts are a mixture of Hereford and Friesian.

Originally Herefords were used as draught animals, pulling wagons and ploughs, until the horse superseded them; and in those days they were all horned. But for nearly a hundred years now there has been a strain of polled Herefords.

Some other less usual breeds of cattle are the Galloway, the Devon, the South Devon, the Sussex, the Welsh Black and the Lincoln Red (their names tell you where you're most likely to find them).

And lastly there are three breeds that are small in numbers but well worth mentioning, because it's rather a thrill to catch sight of them. Each is unmistakable – the Dexter because of its very small size and ridiculously short legs, the Highland because of its long, shaggy, reddish-yellow coat and widespread horns, and the Longhorn, whose name means just what it says.

The Longhorns are the direct descendants of the wild cattle that Stone Age man first domesticated. Large beasts, dark red or roan or brindle but always with a line of white that runs along the back and down the tail, they too were much used as draught oxen in medieval times; at the end of their working lives they were then driven many miles to London's Smithfield Market. Their horns are dramatic, either sweeping forwards or curving downwards and inwards towards the mouth, and they can be well over three feet from tip to tip. I have in my hide a single Longhorn horn which measures two feet from base to point, and that's quite a small one. It was the English Longhorn that settlers took to the New World. Great rangers and good mothers, they were the ideal cattle for the ranchers, and from them came the Texas Longhorns that you see in all the cowboy films.

Longhorn bull

A few years ago, at a famous farm in Gloucestershire where they keep rare breeds of animals, I stood beside a huge Longhorn bull called King. Don't you ever do that. I only did it because I had been assured that I would be quite safe with this particular beast. All the same, when King swung his head at a fly, I jumped a mile.

Never trust a bull, of any breed. (For that matter, never go near a freshly-calved heifer or cow, especially if you've a dog with you, or you may be in trouble.) Bulls of some breeds are quieter than those of others, but even if that old Hereford in the field seems half-asleep, choose another way to go. Even the doziest-looking bull is an immensely powerful animal. Once I had an Aberdeen Angus called Ben. Because like all his kind he was hornless, he could slip his head out of an ordinary cow-chain; so when he came in with the herd at milking-time, he was tied up with a big leather collar like a giant black dog.

One day that collar must have been fixed too loosely or not properly secured. I was out in the yard at the time when suddenly I heard an almighty rending crash, and saw a section of the stout wooden wall of my old-fashioned cowshed burst open as though it had been made of brown paper before the impact of Ben's great head. He stepped through the wreckage and ambled off with a self-satisfied look on his face.

Ben was a 'quiet' bull, but another encounter I had with a bull was not so funny.

It happened at a sale, where the last animal to enter the sale-ring (a flimsy affair of straw bales) was a two-year-old Shorthorn bull. As he was led into the ring, on a bull-pole attached to the ring in his nose, some idiot gave him a tap with a stick and the bull gave a jump and the pole, old and rotten, snapped.

Snorting, blowing, confused and angry, the Shorthorn bull stood in the middle of the circle of straw bales, and with one accord the crowd of buyers made themselves scarce. Every man jack of them – old men, lame men even, moving like lightning – disappeared over fences, up ladders, into the safety of sheds and loose-boxes. Only one dreamy individual remained, goggling, at the ring-side.

The next thing I knew, the bull was coming at speed, head down, his short (but very sharp) horns pointed straight at me.

For the first and only time in my life I experienced the power of flight. I took off and flew through the air like a bird, so strongly that I hit a nearby gate-post with my shoulder and broke it like a rotten carrot, as the Shorthorn bull thundered past, inches away, and galloped off to join the rest of the herd.

Beware of the bull.

There are lots of other 'tame' animals in the countryside, like poultry and pigs, though most of these will be in or near a farmyard rather than running free in the fields. But the animal you're most likely to see, after the sheep and the cow, is the horse.

Horses come in all shapes and sizes, from the little Shetland pony to the huge Shire horse, and very attractive animals they are to most people, to look at, and of course, for many, to ride. I learned to ride ages ago, on a horse called Sturdiboy who was 17½ hands high. A 'hand' is four inches, and the measurement is from the ground to the withers or top of the shoulder; so that meant that Sturdiboy's withers were 5 feet 10 inches from the ground, which looked to me such a long way down that I've never ridden since.

A hundred years ago, before the days of the tractor, all the farmwork was done by horses. Even as recently as 1940 the large Wiltshire farm that I was working on still had a dozen horses in the stable in addition to the tractors. Now it's a rare sight to see horses at work in the field, though happily there are still a few farmers who keep the great heavy breeds – the Shires, the Percherons, the Clydesdales and the Suffolk Punches. We'll need them, they say, if the oil runs out and the tractors (and cars and lorries and trains) can't move.

But if the working horse is rare, the riding horse is not, and in hunting or racing country you'll find plenty of thoroughbreds. And the commonest member of the horse family on view is the pony.

The word 'pony' has nothing to do with the animal's age – a pony doesn't grow up to become a horse. It simply refers to the creature's height. Up to 15 hands (60 inches), it's a pony. Above that, it's a horse. There are eight or nine pure breeds of pony in this country, and one of the most beautiful

Welsh Mountain pony

is the Welsh Mountain. It's small (not usually above 12 hands) and has a lovely head, broad above the big dark eyes and tapering at the muzzle, topped with small, sharply pointed ears. The mane and tail are long and sweeping, and Welsh Mountain ponies come in most colours.

Three other pure native breeds are the New Forest pony, the Dartmoor and the Exmoor. New Forest ponies also have a range of colours; their hind-quarters are rather drooping and their tails set on low. Dartmoor and Exmoor ponies are very tough. They have to be to survive, for in the depths of winter they're out on the moors in the worst of cold and wind and rain and snow. The Exmoor, probably the oldest breed of pony in the British Isles, is fairly distinctive, a mousy-brown colour with a mealy nose and mealy patches round the eyes. And if you see a sturdy little pony with very short legs and a long flowing mane and tail – that'll be a Shetland.

Probably most of the ponies you'll see will be crossbred or out-and-out mongrels, but knowing about and looking out for different colours is interesting. There's quite a range to pick from. Brown and black are just what they say they are, but some of the others need a bit of explaining.

A bay horse, for example, is a lovely, bright, reddish-brown, usually with black legs below the hocks and a black mane and tail.

A piebald has black and white patches of different sizes.

A skewbald has patches of brown (or any colour other than black) and white.

A dun is a sandy colour, often with a darker stripe down the back.

A chestnut has a coat that can be of several shades; some are a bright red-gold, some liver-coloured, and their manes and tails are the same shade as the body or lighter.

A palomino's coat is gold, even yellow, with a silvery or white mane and tail.

A roan is a mixture, as with cattle, of a solid colour with white hairs: chestnut mixed with white – strawberry roan; bay mixed with white – red roan; black mixed with white – blue roan.

You might even find some strangely spotted horses – the Appaloosa is one such breed.

Finally there is grey, an interesting colour that can shade from almost white to nearly black: a very dark grey coat is called 'steel grey'; a white coat with darker rings on it is a 'dapple grey'; and a white coat with brown specks is a 'flea-bitten grey'. Grey foals are usually black at birth, but may end up quite white in old age. By the way, horsy people never talk about a white horse. It's always a grey.

The last domesticated animal you just can't miss is the donkey (I've left it till last, because it's a favourite of mine).

Donkeys haven't the range of colours of horses. They can be blackish, whitish, chocolate or broken-coloured, but usually they're some shade of grey, often with a dark stripe across the shoulders and another down the spine in the shape of a cross. There are four ways in which the donkey differs from the pony. It has small narrow feet, its mane stands up on its neck instead of falling to one side, it has a tuft on the end of its tail and it has very long, narrow ears.

The donkey's other name is the ass, and it has a reputation for stupidity which is completely undeserved. Donkeys are quite intelligent animals. Take comfort from this, next time someone calls you a 'silly ass'. It just means that he's a silly human.

donkey

Chapter 7

HIGHSPEED HIDE

Another sort of hide for observing animals goes along at over 100 m.p.h. And although it's going so fast and making quite a lot of noise, they don't take the slightest notice of it.

It's a highspeed train, and because the creatures that live beside a railway line see so many trains every day of their lives, they aren't a bit disturbed by the speeding monsters.

From your point of view, as an observer, this is a very comfy kind of hide. You simply need to make sure of a seat by the window, and on a journey of any length you're bound to see lots of interesting things. But because you're travelling so fast, you've got to keep your wits about you and your eyes skinned or else you'll miss something.

Here's a list I made, on a recent journey on the InterCity 125. (I just jotted down things in the order in which they turned up.)

Surprise, surprise, a herd of Friesian cows! A large herd, 150 beasts or more (no time to count). Almost all are lying down, cudding. They will have finished their first period of grazing after the morning milking, gathering each mouthful with a twist of the tongue, gripping it and tearing it off with a jerk of the head. All that grass goes straight down into the first of their four stomachs, the rumen or paunch. Now, their paunches full, they are lying down to chew the cud. After about an hour, their paunches will be emptied and up they'll get to graze again. The last few animals are going down as we pass, kneeling first before letting their hindquarters slump down. When they rise again, it will be up on to hindlegs first, different from horses who lie down by gathering their legs under themselves before kneeling and sinking, and, to get up, straighten and rise on to their forelegs first. If I had a pound for every Friesian I shall see today, I'd be a rich man by the time we reach the end of this journey.

Three carrion crows in the middle of a piece of rough rushy pasture, walking about, pecking for grubs. One is a juvenile, this year's bird. I can see this because the young bird approaches one parent with open beak and flaps its wings, begging for food although it's now as big as the adults, and perfectly able to feed itself.

A very old-looking donkey, standing stockstill in an orchard, thinking. Although horses can live a long time (I knew one of thirty-six), donkeys are even longer-lived. An age of forty-seven has been recorded. This one looks pretty ancient. He's sway-backed and his face is very sunken. He doesn't look at the train.

A flight of woodpigeons bursts out of trees beside the line, their white collars, the white bars on their wings and their pinkish breasts bright in the sunshine. They tip away in several different directions, obviously wary of gunshot, for it's nearing harvest-time. They'll be getting even fatter in the yellowing cornfields. You never see a skinny woodpigeon.

Scruffy little pond in corner of field, beside lane below embankment. On it, pair of moorhens and their brood of four chicks, black and still fluffy-looking. As always, the adults, bills bright red with a yellow tip, jerk their heads as they swim. These jerk their tails too, a sign of nervousness, probably at the nearness of the train. Babies imitate these movements.

'Scruffy little pond in corner of field . . .'

I said 'scruffy' because I can see in the pond, as we flash by, tins, plastic bottles and a polythene sack. How sad (and angry) it makes me that people should chuck their rubbish all over the country-side. What are dustbins and litter baskets and dumps for? It's nothing, in our lanes at home, to find old cookers, TV sets, armchairs and sofas, even burnt-out cars.

Stop being sad and angry – at a great piece of luck!
A herd of Longhorns, in a big field right beside the
track. Feel like pulling the communication cord, so
that we can stop and have a good look at these rare
beasts. Only a small herd, perhaps a dozen animals, several with calves (hornless as yet, of
course) at foot. Mostly roans, all with that dis-
tinguishing white line along spine and down tail,
all living up to their name. One has a pair of horns
that curve as though trying to meet in front of her
muzzle. Curiously – perhaps by chance – they are
not, like ordinary cattle, all grazing fairly close
together, in the same direction, but are dotted
about all over the large field. The calf nearest the
track suddenly makes an excited buck-jumping
run. Otherwise the ancient Longhorns take absolutely no notice of the modern 125.

A rabbit! A big one, a buck, I should say, judging
by his large round head. Only a glimpse of him, as
he is hopping slowly along, just outside the railway
fence, doing about one m.p.h. while we're going
over a hundred. Watch carefully for the next minute (during which time the 'hide' has covered the
best part of two miles) for other rabbits, but no
luck.

Now there's a bird that's unmistakable by its flight. It's some distance away, flying between one isolated oak-tree and another in a park-like piece of country, so I can't see it clearly. And I certainly can't hear its distinctive cry – in this hide, unlike my one at home, you can hear nothing of the creatures you see. But I expect it's laughing at something or other – the green woodpecker always does. Though this one's far off, the way that it flies gives away its identity for sure. It's a wavy flight; up, down, up, down, and between each upward bound it closes its wings for quite a little time on the downward swoop before bounding up again. Green woodpeckers are beautiful birds, darkish green above, yellow-rumped and with a brilliant crimson crown, and they are called by a number of different local names. I like 'yaffle', which sounds a bit like its loud echoing laugh.

Another bit of luck – catch sight of a hare. The luck (which all animal watchers need) is of several sorts. First, that the hare should have been so close to the line. Second, that it's in a bare pasture, recently grazed, so that it's clearly visible (squatting, motionless, long ears laid back, looking like a brown clod: I imagine it had been lolloping across the field and had frozen at the train's approach).

Third, that I just happened to be looking in exactly the right place at exactly the right moment to focus upon it, and see, incidentally, that it had a reddish tinge about its shoulders, which makes it likely to be a jack or male. And fourthly, that as it vanished from my sight, I became aware of a voice saying patiently 'Tickets, please'. How many times the collector had already said it to this traveller whose nose was pressed against the window, I don't know, but if I'd heard him earlier I wouldn't have seen my hare.

Talking of the colour of that particular hare reminds me of something very strange. A month or so ago I was walking with Sam, when he suddenly began to cast about, scenting something. I walked on, and from behind a grass tussock right in front of me (so that I know I was not mistaken) a hare got up and slipped away across the hillside, keeping very low, ears flat back.

Nothing strange about that? Oh yes, there was. That hare was the most extraordinary colour. Hares are brown, darker or lighter perhaps, but brown. This hare was orange, the colour of a tangerine! I watched it (Sam didn't see it, and when he found the line, I called him off) for a good ten seconds, and it was exactly the colour of a pet rabbit I once had of a breed called Orange Rex. It must have been a sport, a freak animal – I've never seen a hare like it before and I don't suppose I ever shall again and I don't think anyone believes me, any more than they did about the badger I bashed with my hat.

Must be near a river – a pair of swans flying parallel to us, some distance away so that I have quite a good view of their distinctive flight, long necks outstretched, their wings making (though of course I cannot hear it) that strange, loud, singing note.

These will be Mute swans, the commonest kind. You can tell a Mute swan from a Bewick's or a Whooper by its orange bill with black knob and base. The male is called a cob, the female a pen, and the young ones cygnets. Don't go near a swan's nest in April. The cob will attack you and he can do a lot of harm with a buffet of his powerful wings.

A rather tumbledown farmstead looms up – lots of things to see here, if I can scribble them down quickly enough.

Orchard, with sheep grazing, lambs bigger now than their shorn mothers, a mongrel lot, Heinz sheep (fifty-seven varieties).

Duckpond with interesting ducks (Indian Runners, very long upstretched necks, curious upright waddle), and small flock of geese, the adults white, the goslings as big as their parents but still (as happens with cygnets) darker, woollier-looking in their first plumage.

Tame pigeons sitting on ridgepole of shed, unusual variety called Nuns – white bodies, black heads with a crest at the back.

On a broken wall in front of the shed, a couple of kids are playing (no, not children, young goats, but

'a couple of kids are playing'

they're playing a children's game, King of the Castle). One leaps on to the top of the wall and threatens its brother or sister below with a fierce sweep of its stubby little horns before taking a flying leap down with a show-off twist of its body in mid-air, while the other takes its turn on the castle.

Large flock of rooks striding busily about a field, searching, stabbing the ground. Rooks are good friends to the farmer, eating great quantities of harmful grubs like leather-jackets and wireworms. In return, they charge a modest fee – some of the farmer's seed corn. Unwillingly he pays up, by sowing an extra 'bushel for the birds'.

I can't see the rookery of these particular birds but I know it will differ in one way from the rookeries of my childhood. They were almost always built in elms, the rook's favourite, sometimes as many as forty nests to a tree. The elm was a tall tree with plenty of easily gathered sticks and twigs to make their clumsy but strong nests, stuck together with a bit of mud and lined with grass, sheep's wool and cow's hair. Now the elms are gone and the rooks must use other types of trees, not as tall, not as safe.

A small herd of Jersey cows, grazing busily. One or

two look up as the train whizzes past, staring incuriously at us with big dark eyes. Quite a variety of shades in this herd, from a dark mulberry to a fawn so pale as almost to be grey. Curious thing about Jerseys – when they moult their winter coats they often change colour when the new hair grows, fawn to dun for example.

Kestrel hovering at about forty feet above a patch of rough ground, head bent almost at right angles to body, eyes searching. As we pass, it shuts its wings and drops to earth, but time and the 125 wait for no falcon, and we're gone before there's a chance to see if it's caught anything.

See a single magpie ('one for sorrow') so use my own particular remedy to ward off bad luck: which is to spit at the bird (not a real spit, just a spitty noise) and say, respectfully, 'Good morning, my lord'.

Wonder whether my old tailless friend has survived. I suspect not. Haven't seen him for ages.

Not one, but a whole herd of Shetland ponies, nine or ten of them.

This breeder, whoever he is, is obviously mad on skewbalds. Most of these are brown and white, a couple brown with a belt of white round their middles, making their fat tummies look even fatter. Long manes and tails almost brush the ground as they graze, making short legs look even shorter.

Shetland ponies

Passing a conifer plantation, see a jay flying towards its shelter.

Bird is too distant for me to see its bright colours, but I am sure it's a jay because of its style of flying which is rather heavy and laboured, as though it hadn't long learned the trick. The flight of some birds looks effortless, but the jay always seems to be flapping hard to keep going.

Once you become skilled enough, it's fun to try

to identify the silhouette of a distant bird simply by its flight pattern. And notice how differently birds move on the ground. The starling walks but can hop if it wants to, the woodpigeon's walk is more of a waddle and it's too heavy for hopping, the blackbird makes sudden quick runs between hops, the moorhen only walks, the robin only hops.

There's a robin now, sitting on top of a fence-post right opposite my highspeed hide. It's bobbing up and down on its perch, obviously furious at the nearness of the train to its territory.

How can I see all that as we flash by? I couldn't but we don't. After dashing through the country-side at a breakneck rate (about 120 m.p.h. on some stretches, I should guess) the 125 is now standing motionless, waiting for a signal, I suppose, and this particular robin is extremely angry with it.

Robins are stroppy little birds, and very un-sociable too. The cock only puts up with his mate long enough for breeding and then wants nothing more to do with her. A robin's territorial bound-aries are very exact. I often see two robins hopping up and down either side of an invisible line through the middle of my lawn, no more than a foot apart and cursing each other like mad. This one obvi-ously considers the 125 is trespassing.

Robins are soft-billed insect-eaters, unlike the hard-billed seed-eaters such as sparrows and finches, and the robin is often the early bird that gets the worm. The saying is correct, because worms like the early morning dew, and not hot sunshine.

The train moves, and the angry robin flies away.

Fields disappearing now as we begin to enter a built-up area.

Of course I have seen many animals many times over during this journey without boringly mentioning them each time – woodpigeons, crows, rooks, magpies, sheep, ponies, cows (especially Friesian cows – I'd be about £5,000 richer by now).

We're running in through the suburbs. Soon

we'll be in the heart of a great city. And there too
(just in case you thought animals only lived in the
countryside) we can see a whole host of creatures,
enough to fill another book. If we keep a good
watch.

Chapter 8

TAILPIECE

I'm back at home, sitting in my old hide, looking down over the paddock and up over Burr Acre to the hills beyond.

It's a fairly typical English summer's day, cool, wet and windy, and the overcast sky looks empty, not a single swallow, swift or martin to be seen. The Church Farm herd is standing below me, tails turned to the driving rain (half a tail in one case).

Amongst them hops a solitary magpie, and I'm just about to greet him in the proper manner when a whole family of magpies come flying up the paddock to join him. Six more, making seven in all, and 'Seven's heaven'!

I wish one was my clumsy, awkwardly hopping

friend who'd lost his tail-feathers. I haven't seen him for quite a time. I know he was around for a good few weeks, because he learned to hop into my hen-run, and most days I'd see him in there, pinching chicken-food which I didn't begrudge him, hoping it might help him to grow a new tail.

Maybe he has.

That would make a happy ending, wouldn't it?

BIBLIOGRAPHY

The Young Naturalist's Handbook, by Leonard Moore (Hamlyn, 1978)

Mammals in Britain, by T. Jennings (Adam & Charles Black, 1977)

Spotter's Guide to Animals, Tracks and Signs, by A. Leutscher (Usborne, 1979)

Nature Day and Night, by Richard Adams (Kestrel, 1978)

The Countryside Companion, by Geoffrey Young (Country Life Books, 1985)

The Shell Country Book, by Geoffrey Grigson (Phoenix House, 1962)

Foxes in your Neighbourhood (RSPCA, 1985)

Hedgehogs (RSPCA, 1984)

The Wild Red Deer of Exmoor, by A. Vowles (Cox, Sons & Co. 1936)

Wildlife Begins at Home, by Tony Soper (David & Charles, 1975)

Nature Through the Seasons, by Richard Adams (Kestrel, 1975)

Woodlands, by W. Condry (Collins, 1974)

Everyday Birds, by Tony Soper (David & Charles, 1976)

Badgers, by Ernest Neal (Blandford Press, 1977)

Garden and Field Birds, by J. Felix (Octopus Books, 1974)

The Observer's Book of Birds, by S. V. Benson (Frederick Warne, undated)

The Observer's Book of Wild Animals, by W. J. Stokoe (Frederick Warne, undated)

Farms, by Mary French (Mills & Boon, 1974)

The Real Book of Horses, by Jay Sherman (Dennis Dobson, 1959)

INDEX

Dear Reader,

I hope you've enjoyed reading *Country watch* as much as I've enjoyed writing it. Sadly, many of the animals featured in *Country watch* are fast becoming endangered species. Every year in Great Britain 3 million animals die needlessly, from man made causes.

If we are to preserve some of our wildlife from extinction, we must act now! *But what exactly can we do to help?*

Recently, I was introduced to the work of Les and Sue Stocker. They run a wildlife hospital at their home in Buckinghamshire, and they treat over 4,000 animals a year, including badgers, foxes, toads, swans, rabbits, hedgehogs . . . The list is endless and the Stockers never turn an animal away.

Now the Stockers plan to construct a purpose-built wildlife hospital with top-quality equipment and proper training facilities. They want to be able to help even more animals *and* teach other people how to care for injured wildlife.

The Stockers have been given some land for the hospital, but they need to raise half a million pounds to build it. Tessa Dahl, daughter of Roald Dahl, has been so impressed by the work of Les and Sue, that she has set up the Wildlife Hospital Trust Appeal.

You can make a vital contribution to the appeal by helping them to buy much needed equipment for the new hospital:

£5.00 buys an outside nesting box
£10.00 buys a set of trays, bowls and fittings for an inside cage
£20.00 buys a ceramic heating unit
£30.00 buys an acclimatization hutch
£50.00 buys a complete intensive-care cage

There are all sorts of ways you might be able to raise money for the appeal – perhaps through a sponsored read or swim or by organizing a jumble sale or fête. It's worth talking to your friends or your teachers to see if they have any bright ideas. But whatever you do, and however much money you make for the Wildlife Hospital Trust, I know that every penny will be gratefully received.

If you make a contribution, you will receive a certificate, a letter from the Stockers, a copy of the WHT's magazine and some useful fact sheets on wildlife. If you raise enough money to buy a complete intensive-care cage, it will carry a plaque with your name on it.

I hope you'll join me in helping the work of the hospital.

Any cheques or postal orders should be made payable to The Wildlife Hospital Trust Appeal and sent to:

COUNTRY WATCH, The Wildlife Hospital Trust Appeal, No. 1 Pemberton Close, Aylesbury, Buckinghamshire HP21 7NY.

Thank you.

Dick King-Smith

Some other Puffins

PETS FOR KEEPS
Dick King-Smith

Twelve simple pets, from hamsters to budgies, each with an anecdote, and lots of useful and practical hints for pet owners and also for potential owners.

HOW TO CATCH TIDDLERS
Ian Russell

A humorous, no-nonsense, extensively illustrated approach to tiddler-catching. Instantly accessible to anyone who, with very little equipment, can go and start catching tiddlers immediately.

THE ANIMAL QUIZ BOOK
Sally Kilroy

A heavily illustrated quiz book for around nine-year-olds, covering all kinds of animals, birds, insects and reptiles.